Roses Of All Colors

Dr. Hemendra Kumar Mandal

Chennai • Bangalore

CLEVER FOX PUBLISHING
Chennai, India

Published by CLEVER FOX PUBLISHING 2024
Copyright © Dr. Hemendra Kumar Mandal 2024

All Rights Reserved.
ISBN: 978-93-56487-61-1

This book has been published with all reasonable efforts taken to make the material error-free after the consent of the author. No part of this book shall be used, reproduced in any manner whatsoever without written permission from the author, except in the case of brief quotations embodied in critical articles and reviews.

The Author of this book is solely responsible and liable for its content including but not limited to the views, representations, descriptions, statements, information, opinions and references ["Content"]. The Content of this book shall not constitute or be construed or deemed to reflect the opinion or expression of the Publisher or Editor. Neither the Publisher nor Editor endorse or approve the Content of this book or guarantee the reliability, accuracy or completeness of the Content published herein and do not make any representations or warranties of any kind, express or implied, including but not limited to the implied warranties of merchantability, fitness for a particular purpose. The Publisher and Editor shall not be liable whatsoever for any errors, omissions, whether such errors or omissions result from negligence, accident, or any other cause or claims for loss or damages of any kind, including without limitation, indirect or consequential loss or damage arising out of use, inability to use, or about the reliability, accuracy or sufficiency of the information contained in this book.

CONTENTS

The Mother Instinct 2
The Blue Empress 3
Jingle Bells Jingle Bells 4
The God Is Good 5
Swinging Up And Down 6
When Darkness Is Positive 7
Animal Nature Of Humans 8
Curse Or Blessing Both Are Dreaming 9
The Real Love 10
Limitless Limitations 11
She 12
The Heart From Heaven 14
Tough Outer Tender Inner 15
The Children Of Boldness 16
Friends Forever 17
Peace By Force Is Art 18
The Level Crossing 19
An Ounce Of Practice Is More Than Tons Of Theories 20
Nature Is The Strings Of Violine In My Brain ??? 21
[Christmas Red Birds Sing] 23
The Security Blanket 24
The Warning Whistle 25
The Christmas Day The Sacrifice Day 26
The Body Is A Temple 27
Thunderstorms Without Any Norms 28
Solstice Has Its Nice Poultice 29
Fragrance Is Synonymous To Flowers 30
Hny2022 31

The Beauty Of Old Age	32
The New Year Resolutions	33
The Crazy Boy Of 3 Years	34
Christmas Has A Meaning	35
The Last Journey	36
My Confidence Is The Evidence	37
My Imaginations	38
Alien Thoughts Are Fantastical	39
[God Is Great Magician]	40
Her Vision Of Her Autumn	41
Dreams Of A Child	42
The Taj Mahal The Snatched Siva Temple	43
The Enchanted Boy And The Dog	44
Collaborative Art Inspiration For People	45
Seated In The Grave With Flowers	46
Physically Phoenix	47
Winter Oh You Are Mine !!!!!!	49
Ohh My Country India .. My Diamond Mine	51
The New Year Please Hear My Fear	53
The Heat Of A Cool Winter	55
[Beginning Of End]	56
To Write A Poem	57
At The Dead Of Night	58
Love Is The Same Reflection On Two Hearts' Mirrors	60
Thought For Departing Dad	61
Dancing With Red Signal	62
The Curse Of Flood Was Blessing At Last	63
Money Begets Money	64
Freewheeling Feelings Of Hermits	65
In My Tiresome Evenings	66
We Need To Wage A War Against	68
Amnesia The Bane Of Living	69
The Cool Flowers From A Cool Forest	70
Drag On Ohh Colorful Dragon	71

Contents

The Cautious Heron 72
Living is being and becoming 73
My conditional happiness 74
Blood Built Civilization 75
At The Darkness Of Night 76
Only Truth Exists Others Are Nonexistent 77
Handicrafts 78
Nasty Letter Followed By Nasty Humor 79
Fair Story Of A Beautiful Fairy 80
New Year's New Festive Moods 82
Time The Destiny Of Aging 83
Freewheeling With No Limitations 84
Sense Of The Sensual Love 85
Poetry Is The Life Of A Poet 86
My Ecstatic Flight 87
Dumb Tongue In Succumbed Scenario 89
My Mom The Great Love Bomb 90
Country Girl Is My Pearl 92
Cow Milk Wow Milk!!!!!! 94
Your Magical Touch Was To Me Very Much 95
Transcendental Transgender 96
Gold Is Golden That May Embolden 97
The Dangerous Sea Is Like A Boundless Baby 98
The Running Bride Against The Tide 100
In The Temple On The Mountain 101
As A Doctor My Service To A Poor Cancer Patient 102
I Loved Her One Way 104
Sensuality Of Sensitive Sex 106
Poetic Sublimation For Ultimate Civilization 108
The Fairness Of The Fairy 109
You Are My Love Teacher 110
The Lights Of Darkness 112
The Aliens 113
The Ticking On The Sands Of Time 115

You Chased Me Throughout My Life 116
You Must Know Power Corrupts 117
My Dancing Only For You.. 118
The Darkness Prevails But 119
The Feast By Your Beauty...... 120
Love Is Amazing.. 121
My Poem My Dreams My Love's Chocolate Creams 122
Programed For A Purpose... 123
Love The Greatness Of Goodness... 124
Most Complex Work Is To Be Simple...................................... 125
The Advent Of A Man Of 70 126
Every Sinner Has A Future Every Saint Had A Past.................. 127
Role Of The Oppressed And Oppressors 128
Word Is Omnipotent.. 129
Addiction When It Is A Diction 130
The Hinglish Language... 131
Imprisoned In The Trap Of His Own.. 132
Reincarnation Is A Fact Not Imagination 133
I Could Not Imagine That Day Will Ever Come 134
When Passion Is Compassionate 136
The Scorn Is Born Without Any Mother And Any Norm.......... 137
Hungry And The Old Man 139
The Giggling Baby.. 140
Kids Love Dynamics 141
I Have Got You At Last.. 142
Poets' Role In These Tough Times 143
Waiting For The Day.. 145
I Know But Maybe You Don't 146
Happiness Is Inborn Not Artificially Made............................... 147
World Poetry Day 21st March Dedicated To Long
March For Poets 148
No War Can Be Fought Without Love 150
The Woman Means The Whole Of Civilization......................... 152
The Three Deaths In A Bike Accident....................................... 153

Contents **vii**

Dynamics Of Life Is Brought By War........ 154
Wars Are Play For Leaders As They Aren't Sufferers 156
Ambitious Humans Made Themselves Robots.......................... 158
Daydreaming....Prompt..1 159
When I Was Just A Curious Boy Of 8 Years 160
Faceless Facial.. 161
Bleeding Hearts... 162
Deluge The Earth By Your Mirth 163
My Heart Is Broken Inside 165
If Winter Comes Can Spring Be Far Behind ?...Oscar Wilde..... 166
My Future.... 167
Beauty Is Skin Deep 168
April's Full Entertainment 169
A Naughty Girl 170
The Ordeal Was Where I Was The Witness ,The Cancer............ 172
The Falling Water From Waterfalls 174
Amar Valobasar Asha... 175
The Meditative Afternoon 176
Key Chain 177
We Are Multi Personality 3 In 1 178
Coffee At The Root Of My Brain 179
My Dolls Came From My Love.. 180
Sex Is Not A Taboo Like Drugs 181
But Still.. 182
Eighteen Needs More Freedom 184
Biden Also Born By A Drain 185
Poetry Doesn't Depend On A Particular Month 186
The Bike Accident 187
My Thoughts For You Changed Me Forever ??? 189
To Be The Dear Be Out Of Fear.. 190
Our Encounter With Unprecedented Happiness....................... 191

POEMS BY DR.HUMAN FOR HUMANITY

THE MOTHER INSTINCT

by Dr.Human for humanity on December 17, 2021.
© Dr. Hemendra Kumar Mandal, All rights reserved
When she is mother
She even don't care the father
She has nothing in this world
Except her child and the
Thoughts of it's protection.

THE BLUE EMPRESS

by Dr.Human for humanity on December 17, 2021.
© Dr. Hemendra Kumar Mandal, All rights reserved
She was seated on her throne
Her bright beauty was colorfully grown
She attracted me and all
Around her are white snowballs

She was meditating on others
And others on her
Her beauty took all so far
Forgetting everything they bothered

She is like the Venus
Who has magnetic attraction
Like the flies towards lights
Men were going to her with all their might

JINGLE BELLS JINGLE BELLS……..

by Dr.Human for humanity on December 18, 2021.
© Dr. Hemendra Kumar Mandal, All rights reserved
Very nice and rhythmic song
Impressed me much
It has got my hearts touch
I loved this all along

It induced me to dance
To remember Jesus in his parlance
It is a Christmas Carol
It is great and good for all

I loved Jesus for his bleeding sacrifice
I loved his blessing for all very nice
I loved his disciples for ever
As so much pure in heart they are

My love goes towards the humanity
Expressed by the Christianity
Which induced men like me
To be full of love and without vanity.

THE GOD IS GOOD

by Dr.Human for humanity on December 18, 2021.
© Dr. Hemendra Kumar Mandal, All rights reserved
It is not the everybody's cup of tea
The song is sung on the lyrics of Francesca Battistelli
It was swimming on the tears of the writer
It was the last conclusion of a fighter

It was sung with all the tears
It was sung without fears
God is good but not for all
He is great only who can call

He is submerged in the love of mother
for her baby
He is manifested in the lovers
For the love is so much lovely

He is manifested in prostitutes' cry
He manifested in the birds who can fly
God is good He is great
But to reach him like your kin you must wait

SWINGING UP AND DOWN....

by Dr.Human for humanity on December 18, 2021.
© Dr. Hemendra Kumar Mandal, All rights reserved

Sometimes in my childhood
I was busy in swinging in my playtime
I imagined my legs when up
Touching the blue sky

But when I was down
It was Touching the green grasses
My imagination soured high and low
My pleasure my face was then full of glow

My pleasure went with me
To my home
I used to roam
Always in glee

WHEN DARKNESS IS POSITIVE

by Dr.Human for humanity on December 18, 2021.
© Dr. Hemendra Kumar Mandal, All rights reserved
Sometimes I try to find darkness
To find peace of solitude and loneliness
When I try to discover myself
In my meditation God comes himself

I get my own self manifested
More in darkness than in bright lights
The ghosts are also try to come
But they need some complicated rites

I find also the moonlight magic
Like a silver screen
In my dark corner of my room
Which transport a sleepy dream

The tides also of the sea
Dance in peace in that darkness
All the living beings enjoy peace there
As nobody are there to make them restless.

Light is satisfying its ego
When darkness has its full glow.

ANIMAL NATURE OF HUMANS

by Dr.Human for humanity on December 18, 2021.
© Dr. Hemendra Kumar Mandal, All rights reserved
Humans were meant for refinement
But sometimes they are entangled in
wrong environment
They are created by God to be his kin

He becomes hungry for food
He becomes like animals at times
In his sex hungry mood
Then he becomes hungry for flesh

When he is hungry for days
He finds food with the dogs
In the dustbins
And travel like Mads

He becomes sometimes like snakes
Eating flesh of his fellow races
At times with other animals
He is compelled to drink water at bad places.

sometimes he discover his ignorance
And mends himself in light of goodness.

CURSE OR BLESSING BOTH ARE DREAMING

by Dr.Human for humanity on December 18, 2021.
© Dr. Hemendra Kumar Mandal, All rights reserved
Artist is the reflection of this society
As you sow so you reap a lot
So don't criticize them in entirety
Sometimes blessings Sometimes not

Artist painting with black and white
But he never fights
He also paints with colors
What he thinks absolutely right.

They are the followed of truth
They are holding the cross
They are crystal clear and smooth
They are their own boss.

THE REAL LOVE

by Dr.Human for humanity on December 18, 2021.
© Dr. Hemendra Kumar Mandal, All rights reserved
The real love is always epic
It shakes the world of both very quick
It is impatient for kiss and enjoy
Each other mad for ever.

LIMITLESS LIMITATIONS

by Dr.Human for humanity on December 20, 2021.
© Dr. Hemendra Kumar Mandal, All rights reserved
Yes we always do our work under pressure
We are enjoying freedom but not in great true sense
We are always cornered by innumerable factors
Man is born free but everywhere he is in chains

While we go to shopping my decision is cornered
Whenever I eat for myself my wishes are neglected
My choice of tourist places are dominated by wife
To be good for families and friends I had to sacrifice

Mom have to sacrifice for children
Husbands have to sacrifice for wife
As the Jesus had to sacrifice his life
Everybody meant to sacrifice to survive

SHE

by Dr.Human for humanity on December 20, 2021.
© Dr. Hemendra Kumar Mandal, All rights reserved

Yes she was the magic
she was the tragic music
Influenced my mind
She was of a unique kind

She mesmerized me on the road
On the platform
She was alone but full of load
Of exquisite form

I could not but focus on her
As every step of her is better
Than the earlier
She was a colorful rumor

She was criticized by all
But nobody could avoid her call
She was not prostitute
she was not good but you must fall to her charismatic call.

I had to bear her nuisance
I had to enjoy her pursuance
I had to become her dog
No options were there for me as she was my God.

THE HEART FROM HEAVEN

by Dr.Human for humanity on December 20, 2021.
© Dr. Hemendra Kumar Mandal, All rights reserved
Yes I think so her heart is made at heaven
By the hand of God with the mother's feelings
To everyone to baby to a old man
Her heart is bleeding always like mother Mary

I felt her heart while loving her under the tree
She was so cool and so much free
She kissed me very soft on my lips
Her warm hugs was to me full of bliss

Without her I was alone
Like the children Without the mom
She sent me boundless love
I thought sometimes she is in my heart

LIKE THE GOD ABOVE........

TOUGH OUTER TENDER INNER

by Dr.Human for humanity on December 23, 2021.
© Dr. Hemendra Kumar Mandal, All rights reserved
The warriors are peculiar kind of mortals
Tough exteriors but soft interiors
As if you can't love your nation you can't do that job
Basically a lover for his motherland's heartthrob

A disciplined life a streamlined strife
Don't care the bleeding life
Don't care own family and friends
Only to protect his nation and lands

The attractive life the call of the love
He shuns everything only for the nation
Fighting with the cruel nature with the nature's call
He can give up even himself above all

His vision his mission when getting old
Still He is the guard of the honor and bold
He is the power behind every attack to the enemy
Streamlined with his powerhouse of all energy.

THE CHILDREN OF BOLDNESS

by Dr.Human for humanity on December 23, 2021.
© Dr. Hemendra Kumar Mandal, All rights reserved
We need you in every walks of life
Fighting is the order of the day
Everywhere is strife
Fighting only can make your way

The blood running through your veins
The world always trains
Your mind with every kind of war sense
Towards the static and useless brains

The warrior on the fields
Always new way he builds
For the hope of mankind
For the new light of a brighter mind

Every fighter has one thing common
They sacrifice their life for others not his own
The don't think the consequence
They can't be selfish with their pure innocence.

FRIENDS FOREVER

by Dr.Human for humanity on December 23, 2021.
© Dr. Hemendra Kumar Mandal, All rights reserved
Friends are a peculiar kind of mortals
As I always think over their portals
They are full of helping hands indeed
Their good wishes always stand in need.

They are lovers of pure heart
They are fighters for compassion
They always have a good start
To encourage your mind's reccssion

PEACE BY FORCE IS ART

by Dr.Human for humanity on December 24, 2021.
© Dr. Hemendra Kumar Mandal, All rights reserved
I know a professional murderer
Suddenly in love to a next door neighbor
The lady loved him, I don't know what's her goal
But she gave every effort to control.

THE LEVEL CROSSING

by Dr.Human for humanity on December 24, 2021.
© Dr. Hemendra Kumar Mandal, All rights reserved
The cow was adamant to cross the railway line
As there was nice green grass
But the train was passing just then
The guard on the gate tried to control

The people surrounding screaming
Please don't let it go
Because the immediate danger is on his way
The guard was busy signaling the train

The cow was concentrated on the grass
Not anything more
Lastly it was called with some food
By the guard to avoid the immediate death

I was at dismay what to do or not to
But I was pleased about the humanity
Shown by all the crowd and the gate man
They were too much concerned to be a kind human

AN OUNCE OF PRACTICE IS MORE THAN TONS OF THEORIES

by Dr.Human for humanity on December 26, 2021.
© Dr. Hemendra Kumar Mandal, All rights reserved
we have expended tons of words
From our cozy drawing room
Tons of words are preached by the
Peace prize winners but to no effect

Merely weeping for injured animals
Painful animal never makes this earth more peaceful
Please step down to the streets and forests
to love them live.......

NATURE IS THE STRINGS OF VIOLINE IN MY BRAIN ???

by Dr.Human for humanity on December 26, 2021.
© Dr. Hemendra Kumar Mandal, All rights reserved
A love of nature keeps no factories busy....Aldous Huxley, Brave new world...

When reach to my nature's lap
I think it's my own and not others
Freewheeling as I go there
The twittering birds without depressions

I become instantly free without loneliness
When I gaze to the pearls on the grasses
Glittering with the dawn's own golden sunshine
I then only can break all the frontiers

I can only then go to heavenly feels devoid of me
To the Huxley's Brave new world
Full of confidence built upon myself
With the strong and bold blue waves on the shore

I find eternal joy only then in exclusion with nature
Which can only be found by the poets who are
Drunken only by their creations
Nothing more nothing less,
The remainders let's guess……..

[CHRISTMAS RED BIRDS SING]

by Dr.Human for humanity on December 26, 2021.
© Dr. Hemendra Kumar Mandal, All rights reserved
christmas red birds sing
the winter snow looks
the nature's calling all
god is looking from behind

THE SECURITY BLANKET

by Dr.Human for humanity on December 29, 2021.
© Dr. Hemendra Kumar Mandal, All rights reserved
To the piercing winter
Your hugs were just like a security cover
To protect me with your cozy love
Just like the warm winter sun above

Even I was very cold
Then your lust was very bold
Which at the same time satiated me
With hot enjoyment that made me free

You were always my guide to the pleasure patch
Which surely made me for your match
Your loving blanket cover
Always wanted me to discover

The final meaning of careless pleasure

THE WARNING WHISTLE

by Dr.Human for humanity on December 29, 2021.
© Dr. Hemendra Kumar Mandal, All rights reserved
That is the edge which always warns me
You are at your end of a life which is carefree
I am compelled then to control my plan further
My pleasure then instructs me not to go that far

When I become drunk enough to forget I drank what for
What is the festival what is the enjoyment
The the edge comes in front of me as final door
Which is enough to make me silent.

THE CHRISTMAS DAY THE SACRIFICE DAY

by Dr.Human for humanity on December 29, 2021.
© Dr. Hemendra Kumar Mandal, All rights reserved
The Christmas day is a very special day
The churches are adorned In a new bride's way
The cakes and drinks and juices galore
We celebrate with a merry heart more and more

We celebrate the sacrifice day with family and parents
The fruits and cakes are distributed to the patients
The Christmas Carol are sung in a flying mood
The life of Jesus is thought and understood

The disciples life are commemorated
The bands and musics are repeated
Till the dawn till the Joy became unbounded
Long live Jesus we call from heart unbridled.

THE BODY IS A TEMPLE

by Dr.Human for humanity on December 30, 2021.
© Dr. Hemendra Kumar Mandal, All rights reserved
The body is an instrument for my works
It is in a showcase to show my focus
It's my creative window pane
So I need it to properly maintain

It must be functioning in my bad days
It must help me in my good ways
It should help me to meditate
It should accompany me to contemplate

It will go with my sports
It must be fit to overcome my owes
So it must not be obese
It should never be useless

It should be void of diseases
It must go along in my pleasure and pain
It helps me to worship truth and beauty forever
Otherwise it's all in vain.

THUNDERSTORMS WITHOUT ANY NORMS

by Dr.Human for humanity on December 31, 2021.
© Dr. Hemendra Kumar Mandal, All rights reserved

The snow balls were grown
The calamities were on
The natural beauty has gone wild
When just came the blizzard
Mighty blow
By the snow
Made me alone.....

SOLSTICE HAS ITS NICE POULTICE

by Dr. Human for humanity on December 31, 2021.
© Dr. Hemendra Kumar Mandal, All rights reserved

The great coverage by the solstice
In the coldest winter day
With the festive mood people dance it away
The spirit is high-flying

Warm hearts don't care
The coolest threat amidst blow of snow fare
They make it happen to enjoy
The festivities in a colorful convoy

Humans are a race who always
Challenges the wars by the nature
With an awesome dignity
And prepares a conquering altar

FRAGRANCE IS SYNONYMOUS TO FLOWERS

by Dr.Human for humanity on December 31, 2021.
© Dr. Hemendra Kumar Mandal, All rights reserved
My idea of fragrance is rooted to flowers
The poets' ideas of fragrance are flowers
The ideas of my beautiful colors are flowers
So my fountainhead of beauty is flowers

The serotonin of my brain is flowers
My medication of depression is flowers
My imagination of perfume is flowers
My lover is compared to flowers

My marriage was covered by flowers
My carriage there was decorated by flowers
I lost my mind in the flowers
My songs are careless with flowers

HNY2022

by Dr.Human for humanity on December 31, 2021.
© Dr. Hemendra Kumar Mandal, All rights reserved
The future is to come
Once again for new hopes
Good to come and bad to go

THE BEAUTY OF OLD AGE

by Dr.Human for humanity on December 31, 2021.
© Dr. Hemendra Kumar Mandal, All rights reserved
The age is going down the lane
To travel to the unknown
He is full of worldly knowledge
And experience more than a college

He is accepted by all
Children, young, short and tall
Respected by beautiful girls and boys
He is cool and devoid of noise

He is consulted by all
As he is getting tall
Day by day
On his way

When he is strolling to the setting sun
at the dusk for a walk
His shadow reminds him again
You are above all this worldly pain.

THE NEW YEAR RESOLUTIONS

by Dr.Human for humanity on January 1, 2022.
© Dr. Hemendra Kumar Mandal, All rights reserved
I don't believe in resolutions
As it's rather theoretical than practical ones
It's like promises of politicians
Just framed for votes and none

I believe in being and becoming happy now and here
I believe in actions before promises fare
As I am not politicians so I don't care
I believe in motivations not resolutions

After resolutions are taken in pen and paper
Never they are paid any heed so far
The people agitate but all in vain
They are inflicted ample pain

We go by our ego by our tempo
Not by any plan
So no plan can instigate our motion
Only love for a thing or person can.

Author notes
Word count 110 words

THE CRAZY BOY OF 3 YEARS

by Dr.Human for humanity on January 2, 2022.
© Dr. Hemendra Kumar Mandal, All rights reserved
The angry boy wanted his mom's lap
But rejected
So he directly hit to the breast of his mom
Sitting beside him

She laughed with a little anger
And just cleaned it with a puff.....

CHRISTMAS HAS A MEANING

by Dr.Human for humanity on January 3, 2022.
© Dr. Hemendra Kumar Mandal, All rights reserved
It's not a mere celebration
It's a matter of resolution
Taken for self life and lives of others as well
The sacrifice of Jesus must be the guide as a whole

The colors The pomp the music
Are all in vain
if we don't contemplate
Jesus pain

The birth of a legend
And his life's painful end
Must fill our feelings
That will only make us a more human things

The babies the fathers and mothers
The lovers and sisters and brothers
All should feel the love preached by HIM
Then only the civilization will be more neat and clean

THE LAST JOURNEY

by Dr.Human for humanity on January 3, 2022.
© Dr. Hemendra Kumar Mandal, All rights reserved
The death is our last journey over
Just imagine the coffin with white cover
A procession is marching behind
With flowers and heavy mind

Family and friends
Remember the ends
No more sounds silence
Only remains

The cemetery was ready
under the long woods
A pathetic scenario was steady
Only the passers-by brood....

MY CONFIDENCE IS THE EVIDENCE

by Dr.Human for humanity on January 4, 2022.
© Dr. Hemendra Kumar Mandal, All rights reserved
Yes my life is best when
I am at the top of the world
My feelings are crazy then
but still they are bold

I feel the joy of self-respect

MY IMAGINATIONS

by Dr.Human for humanity on January 4, 2022.
© Dr. Hemendra Kumar Mandal, All rights reserved
As I am tired of practical life
I enjoy imaginations

ALIEN THOUGHTS ARE FANTASTICAL

by Dr.Human for humanity on January 4, 2022.
© Dr. Hemendra Kumar Mandal, All rights reserved
The concept of aliens and UFOs
Really fantastical within the borderline of
Imaginations and realities
About their life and intelligences
Really astonishing!!!!!!!

[GOD IS GREAT MAGICIAN]

by Dr.Human for humanity on January 4, 2022.
© Dr. Hemendra Kumar Mandal, All rights reserved

God is great magician
who plays with colors
beyond my thoughts

HER VISION OF HER AUTUMN

by Dr.Human for humanity on January 5, 2022.
© Dr. Hemendra Kumar Mandal, All rights reserved
She was sitting under the park trees
Brooding with her past her love her warmth
Her heart was full of cosy feels
While the golden glow of sun reels

Her eyes were traveling too far
In a wonderland
The park animals were looking her
As if a foreign object in a foreign land

The cool blanket wrapped over her
At the dusk of the day
A number of leaves falling over
In a trembling way

The autumn induced in her mind
The past love life and memories
Which made her standstill and enshrined
Into a warm sphere of memories

DREAMS OF A CHILD

by Dr.Human for humanity on January 5, 2022.
© Dr. Hemendra Kumar Mandal, All rights reserved

Playfulness is a child
Dreams of naughty plans
Are born out of his sling
The fun is discovered instantly

In his genius plays seriously
life and death thrown away playfully

THE TAJ MAHAL THE SNATCHED SIVA TEMPLE

by Dr.Human for humanity on January 6, 2022.
© Dr. Hemendra Kumar Mandal, All rights reserved
The Taj mahal was not the symbol of love
What the truth described by the archeologists
It was built in the 13th century 300 years before
The reign of Shah Jahan a purely and robust temple

The God of destruction and Universe
Constructed by a Hindu emperor
Which was snatched by force from him
By Shah Jahan for making a memorial

It has a great hall of musicians
Behind the temple to sing for the great lord
No cemetery never had such a musicians place
Alongside the great construction

History has been changed intentionally
To malign the hindu civilization
And uplift the muslim mughal emperors
So Taj mahal is always the Abode of God

And it's permanent as the God Himself.

THE ENCHANTED BOY AND THE DOG

by Dr.Human for humanity on January 6, 2022.
© Dr. Hemendra Kumar Mandal, All rights reserved
The didn't care the external world
While they were enjoying the dance
While their moods were trance
They were careless and bold

They didn't care their faces
The didn't care their dresses
They had hearts very warm
They felt for the other to enjoy

They never needed a convoy to show
Still Their faces were aglow
Rhythmic were They to the tune of their brains
Joy and woe of other worlds were simply ignored

Their love for each other
Didn't help them anything to bother
Their feelings for each
Enchanted them without speech

Author notes
Word count 93 words

COLLABORATIVE ART INSPIRATION FOR PEOPLE

by Dr.Human for humanity on January 6, 2022.
© Dr. Hemendra Kumar Mandal, All rights reserved
Any form of art is universal
Without any language for communication
It's effect is colossal
It has a heart to heart version

It's a language that can be communicated to all
For every reasons and every seasons spring to fall
The colors are the colors of life
With every punch of peace and strife

The artists as well as people
Glued to its clarion call
Crowds come to view one and all
The attraction of it year round spring to fall

Author notes
Word Count 81 words

SEATED IN THE GRAVE WITH FLOWERS

by Dr.Human for humanity on January 7, 2022.
© Dr. Hemendra Kumar Mandal, All rights reserved

We are sometimes
Contradict our feelings
Seated in the Graves
But still acting as we are flowering

This hypocrisy reaches us nowhere
Like contradictory thoughts
We are spinning in the same circle
We get humiliations everywhere

Author notes
36 words

PHYSICALLY PHOENIX

by Dr.Human for humanity on January 7, 2022.
© Dr. Hemendra Kumar Mandal, All rights reserved
So to say we are physically Phoenix
Our body have all the tricks
To treat our problems in the form of disease
It can itself tries to fix

Voltaire the philosopher
Felt the truth
As a body we are smooth
Perfection is present now and here

As we are the blend of body and soul
Some diseases are treated by body in full
And some are treated by our soul
Lastly we become cool

The self within our brains
Always tries and trains
Our white blood cells
Now and then excels

So like faith heeling
We are healed by our own
Body and mind and soul
And we reach in this way to our goal

WINTER OH YOU ARE MINE !!!!!!

by Dr.Human for humanity on January 8, 2022.
© Dr. Hemendra Kumar Mandal, All rights reserved
I am a homesick
I enjoy my home sweet home
I enjoy myself in winter alone
The cool calm quite meditative

The snows are beautiful for happiness
The season of Jesus and Christmas no less
The season of gifts and cakes
The reason of cozy quilts and beds

The season of enjoyment of sleeping
The reasons of Santa coming
The season of fleeing of militants
For the fear of snowfalls

The reasons of love makings
The season of sleeping careless
The season of the hibernation feelings
The reason of the reptiles peaceful easy access

Season to meet friends and lovers
The visions of Jesus and Christmas adores
The decorations of churches and homes
All in one here in winter alone.......

OHH MY COUNTRY INDIA .. MY DIAMOND MINE

by Dr.Human for humanity on January 8, 2022.
© Dr. Hemendra Kumar Mandal, All rights reserved
I could never find another country
In the world with so much riches
For which races and nations conquered us
Some looted and gone some came to live here free

Not only the material riches galore
Here I get the best culture of mind
The sages and philosopher so kind
They taught us life's lessons more and more

It's the country of Aryan and Vedas
The country of knowledge for bliss
The country of Buddha and peace
Here the ramkrishna and vivekananda taught us

Joy of living without nothing
Here meditation made us king
Here the Krishna of Isckon flourished
The good reigned and bad vanquished

All nations came here to get life's knowledge
As this is the permanent freedom from our bondage

THE NEW YEAR PLEASE HEAR MY FEAR

by Dr.Human for humanity on January 9, 2022.
© Dr. Hemendra Kumar Mandal, All rights reserved
I got resolutions year after year
To no effect till now
I became tired by sweat and tear
But couldn't find to reach there how

So not the least but at last
I abandoned my promises to keep fast
I need more than one year to reach my goal
So what I think for this year I don't express it to all

So for now I am disgusted to think over it
To think over fallible promises to keep
I want to work and play but without care
I want to bath in color but without fear or favor

I want to reach that girl
Who can be exchanged by diamond and pearl
But after the year I still have to go a long way
My resolutions were scattered on my way

So don't ask me friends any more
If I have resolutions galore
Even if I have anything more
I am unable those to explore

THE HEAT OF A COOL WINTER

by Dr.Human for humanity on January 9, 2022.
© Dr. Hemendra Kumar Mandal, All rights reserved
I am not in a hibernation
But still I am hot with your hugs
With a moon full winter night outside
I am full of your magical drugs

The mountains with snow are aglow
But in my cozy room heat has a show
The reptiles, lizards are no more here
This winter they never care

The forests the dawn and dusk roads
Resting alone as they have no loads
On their space
Barring a few sunny hours nobody has any trace.

[BEGINNING OF END]

by Dr.Human for humanity on January 9, 2022.
© Dr. Hemendra Kumar Mandal, All rights reserved
beginning of end
is much below mystery
try to recommend

TO WRITE A POEM

by Dr.Human for humanity on January 11, 2022.
© Dr. Hemendra Kumar Mandal, All rights reserved

To write a poem you must be cool
Otherwise danger will make you fool
Your balance of temperament is necessary
You must maintain a nice soul

You must be sensitive to the colors of nature
You should fly with the birds very very far
You must mingle with the golden sunshine
You should go to the blue sea and diamond mine

You must collect gems for your readers
You should guide the useless leaders
You must give peace to the broken lovers
By your poems of hopes to cover up their lives dangers.......

AT THE DEAD OF NIGHT

by Dr.Human for humanity on January 11, 2022.
© Dr. Hemendra Kumar Mandal, All rights reserved

Now I have nowhere to go
Except sitting on my study table
with my thoughts flow
Piercing like a rocket through my window

Engulfed by my vivid colors of thoughts
Some covered by pleasures some by pains
The slept world has many dark spots
Temporarily covered by transient stains

Sleep is working like a balm
It makes ourselves cool and calm
Our disgusting life gets for a while
A medium to forget all those with dreams of smile

I was thinking of those who are in jail
Or those who are in lovers lap without fail
Or those whose life has become a terror
With some of his or her error

Who are taking resort to this dead of night
Forget to fight for life instead go to do suicide
Loveless girls are crying in their bed
Without any information to her lost beloved.

The prisoners declared to be hanged tomorrow
Have the last night to follow the life's blood
Their friends and families with endless sorrow
Their moms are inundated by the tears flood.

LOVE IS THE SAME REFLECTION ON TWO HEARTS' MIRRORS

by Dr.Human for humanity on January 13, 2022.
© Dr. Hemendra Kumar Mandal, All rights reserved
My expectations are reflected on yours
So also your expectations on myself
My smile is your smile
Your style is my style

My fashion is your expectation
As well as your fashion approved by me
Your fragrance engulfed my thoughts
My enjoyments centered on your beauty spots

When we both sing in a chorus resonates
The eternal love exudes heavenly elixirs
Our travel our joy is found in each other
The life itself is fulfilled of both to too far

THOUGHT FOR DEPARTING DAD

by Dr.Human for humanity on January 13, 2022.
© Dr. Hemendra Kumar Mandal, All rights reserved
Today is the day when they divorced with consent mom
and dad, they are happy by snatching mine
How I will miss them they don't want to know
I feel my pain left alone, feel the severe blow

God save me please
As I have to live as a small child ....

DANCING WITH RED SIGNAL

by Dr.Human for humanity on January 13, 2022.
© Dr. Hemendra Kumar Mandal, All rights reserved

Her brave dance with subtle accuracy
Is a source of enjoyable efficacy
Her beauty is the bonus
Her temper is omnivorous

Her caricatures are enjoyable
She is flamboyant as a fable....

THE CURSE OF FLOOD WAS BLESSING AT LAST

by Dr.Human for humanity on January 13, 2022.
© Dr. Hemendra Kumar Mandal, All rights reserved
The river was roaring at the point of death
The banks of it was full of mud at rest
It blown all the projects beside it
Fate taken away everything good and nice

But the soil became very supple
The farming after the calamity
Was too much flourished with stability
The bane was bliss against pain

The next year was of topmost production
What flood snatched from all returned again
People were happy after the curse
They were blessed by the God more than the loss...

MONEY BEGETS MONEY

by Dr.Human for humanity on January 14, 2022.
© Dr. Hemendra Kumar Mandal, All rights reserved
I must roll it through the civilization
As money can only bring money
It's a kind of capital investment
Towards the growth of self reliance

For the poor for the downtrodden
For their upbringing of confidence
The education cycle which can make man
Out of this millions of dollars

Who in turn must take oath to
Spend money to train another million
In this way in this passion
Man making machines will take motion

Billions of dollars will ignite billions of humans
Billions of confident people making strong nations

FREEWHEELING FEELINGS OF HERMITS

by Dr.Human for humanity on January 15, 2022.
© Dr. Hemendra Kumar Mandal, All rights reserved
If we want the best idea about finding happiness
See the life of a hermit on the Himalayas
The don't care any support for three basic necessities
Food, clothes and house for living

As they are careless being full of consciousness
Of the God all the time 24/7
If you see them you must think as if
You are dreaming some unbelievable dreams

Their lives are transformed to a miracle
To the common man
Who can never think of how they live
In the snow and blizzards of the Himalayas!!!!!

IN MY TIRESOME EVENINGS

by Dr.Human for humanity on January 16, 2022.
© Dr. Hemendra Kumar Mandal, All rights reserved
When I am exhausted in the evening
After the day's struggle for living
I need your solace to my heart
All day long the heat of life broken me apart.

My endeavor to gather worldly peace
Ultimately needed one and only your bliss
My friend and foe always try to grow
Enmity and give useless blow

For their selfish ends they try hard
They don't care others problems
They are free to move away after their awards
From my corner to their cozy dens.

In that scenario I felt their harder hearts
Then I feel your bliss in those deserts
I think my heaven is far from those kith and kin
Where I must come at last the peace to win

My tired evenings are dedicated to you
After a day's long journey at last
Nobody could quench my thirst
Except your vibrant and cool view.

WE NEED TO WAGE A WAR AGAINST

by Dr.Human for humanity on January 16, 2022.
© Dr. Hemendra Kumar Mandal, All rights reserved
Yes too many gentlemen spoil the broth
We must take a strong oath
To eradicate the hooligans
To annihilate the criminals

Otherwise a flood of tears will not be enough
To protect our offsprings from the life which is tough
From the guns below and panic above
Some cruel punishment is needed which must be rough.

The victims of depressions take up the gun
Towards the innocent children on the run
People along with the government
Must be qualified to apply capital punishment.

Then the paying homage and weeping for them
Will be enough to handle this kind of mayhem.
Otherwise the hyenas get loose
To the innocent victims with bloody noose.

AMNESIA THE BANE OF LIVING

by Dr.Human for humanity on January 18, 2022.
© Dr. Hemendra Kumar Mandal, All rights reserved
She told her octogenarian husband
To buy some food from market
He went there to take some sanitizer and masks
But she was very angry on these

She told him I wanted you a packet of cigarettes
Why you can forget all those things
Within a short while
They both are living alone in the house nobody to look after

Amnesia is taking its toll to the old people
Without any medical treatments to come
They are both helpless and hapless
In this world of carelessness

May God bless them with some help
May God send them some pure hearts
May God sooth their brains from torture
May God help them with a better future

THE COOL FLOWERS FROM A COOL FOREST

by Dr.Human for humanity on January 20, 2022.
© Dr. Hemendra Kumar Mandal, All rights reserved
Under the sun the playing flowers run
With the wind of the winter and autumn
Colors are bright all the day and night
The passers by have a panoramic sight

The bees fly with their humming sound
Turn by turn moving gleefully going around
The squirrels are looking back and forth
With their energetic jumps and running both

Butterflies trying to circumvent
They take the pollens and enjoying the scent
The cool breeze are passing to and fro
The long and green grasses try nicely to grow.

DRAG ON OHH COLORFUL DRAGON

by Dr.Human for humanity on January 20, 2022.
© Dr. Hemendra Kumar Mandal, All rights reserved
In my fantasy and scores of colors
Dragon lives like the glittering stars
Many stories are running around
In my sleep and waking with roaring sound

The mythological scent is always in the air
When I study stories comes it's flair
The children want to hear more
The strength and magical events galore

The play they go ups and downs
With mystical and magical sounds
The fires are vibrant in the children's eyes
They get much more fear but still they think it nice

THE CAUTIOUS HERON

by Dr.Human for humanity on January 20, 2022.
© Dr. Hemendra Kumar Mandal, All rights reserved
Around the water space
There is no trace of fishes
But with one legged attention
Heron is always fishing fan

The unflinching concentration
The pinpointed motivation
Make it odd man out from the water body
It's sweet and smart style is a unique melody

The eyes are like that of a philosopher
The meditation for fish is going too far
Having Visions To reach the end of the pond
The long beak and the substrate has unbreakable bond.......

LIVING IS BEING AND BECOMING

by Dr.Human for humanity on January 20, 2022.
© Dr. Hemendra Kumar Mandal, All rights reserved

We are sent by God
Here to grow and fight
We must travel always here and abroad
Our way must be honest and right

Live is not only resides with danger
But it also gives us knowledge to be better
Darkness on our way asks us to get the light
Then fighting always with all our might

Sometimes pleasures come our way
Sometimes life causes pain
But we should not go away
From our goals or living will be in vain

MY CONDITIONAL HAPPINESS

by Dr.Human for humanity on January 21, 2022.
© Dr. Hemendra Kumar Mandal, All rights reserved
I am happy when Linda always is my friend
I am happy when beautiful poems she sent
I am happy in the advent of spring
I am happy when the twittering birds sing

I am happy at the odd hours of the day
When my love is coming on my way
When the sea is roaring like a lioness
My happiness get high with her vibrant dress

I am cool and calm with the sunny dawn view
I am astonished with the green grasses dazzling dew
I get happiness with my embracing dog
I get enchanted by the love of lord

I always miss my lovers wet kiss
Her emotions comes to me like a devastating bliss.
Even my happiness comes permanently when I think of HIM
Then my father in the heaven comes in my dream.

BLOOD BUILT CIVILIZATION

by Dr.Human for humanity on January 22, 2022.
© Dr. Hemendra Kumar Mandal, All rights reserved

She is the artist
She is the poet
She is the creator
She is the builder

She is the player
With the blood full river
Into her womb
To bring forth her creation

She wants to paint
To enjoy the colors
The reddish mood of her
Makes her beautiful lover

AT THE DARKNESS OF NIGHT

by Dr.Human for humanity on January 22, 2022.
© Dr. Hemendra Kumar Mandal, All rights reserved
You are beautiful but liked darkness always
Your perversion is your naughty base
But still the people peep on your dress
They enjoy your beauty not anything less

They like you but you don't
As they want to balance both good and bad
Because they are afraid of their dad

Author notes
Wc 50

ONLY TRUTH EXISTS OTHERS ARE NONEXISTENT

by Dr.Human for humanity on January 23, 2022.
© Dr. Hemendra Kumar Mandal, All rights reserved
How can we go after the fantasies of our brains
When truth is available at our sense
We are on the ground level of our base
Falsifying anything I'd merely useless..

If we call a sun as a star
We cannot go too far
We cannot understand the basic difference
Between the sense and the nonsense

We are always cordoned by the wrong
False concepts are leading us along
The road to utter confusion
We know all that but still cannot deny that motivation.

HANDICRAFTS

by Dr.Human for humanity on January 23, 2022.
© Dr. Hemendra Kumar Mandal, All rights reserved
Really our hand can stand on its own
The eternal creation of culture and civilization
Comes through the machinery of our brains
The varieties of our dance are fruits of our hands

But no one probably written an ode to this creator
Nobody thought so down to earth and deep.
As a poet can do in the dreams of his sleep
God one of best creation is our hands indeed

NASTY LETTER FOLLOWED BY NASTY HUMOR

by Dr.Human for humanity on January 25, 2022.
© Dr. Hemendra Kumar Mandal, All rights reserved
Today you will find nasty people around
Cowards galore they can't be bound
To the truth they want to specify
They want to tell the fact but don't identify

The letter is written with an utter anger
But not brave enough, they are
To leave there
Their signature

What a blend of cowardice and fear
What a car without gear
Prone to the immediate accident
Death can only have power to mend them.

FAIR STORY OF A BEAUTIFUL FAIRY

by Dr.Human for humanity on January 25, 2022.
© Dr. Hemendra Kumar Mandal, All rights reserved
Within the forest of a half day half night view
With the calm and cool scene she dropped new
Nobody is there, no sound except the waterfalls
She came to enjoy the beautiful scenario over-all

Under the sky and above the greens
Her innocent heart has so many dreams
To make them true
With her heart trying to pursue

The touching the feeling of cool water
Coming from the fountain near her
Made her giggle made her joyful
She thought she is the queen and came to rule

Her royal gesture Her beautiful wings
Made her so cool with heavenly feelings
The dears with their big eyes came near her
How can she go leaving them too far??!!!

But still she came from heaven
She has to go back their again
She pines for the beauty of this earth
And her heart has got here a new birth !!!!

NEW YEAR'S NEW FESTIVE MOODS

by Dr.Human for humanity on January 26, 2022.
© Dr. Hemendra Kumar Mandal, All rights reserved

The grand gala festivals
Were all around all colors
With baby to elders
From beloved to lovers

Decorations galore
Enjoyment more and more
Lighting in the dark
Gets frequent starry spark

Foods and drinks and dancers
Are in full swing with Jesus answers
Of the spiritually singing moods
All have many many different goods

With hue and cry in the winter's sky
Celebration is getting high
The x Mas trees are in flying colors
The Decorations are full of scented flowers.

TIME THE DESTINY OF AGING

by Dr.Human for humanity on January 27, 2022.
© Dr. Hemendra Kumar Mandal, All rights reserved
Aging is a part of aging
The old man is a cold man shivering
Not a bold man but nearing
The death is coming near to him

The colors of life from red blue and green
Transformed to yellow, white and gray which mean
You are rejected from your target
Your own people has nothing for you and they forget

You are crooked now as time passed
You are nearing the brim of life very fast
Nobody can save you except the time machine
Pray to God for getting your final blessing.....

FREEWHEELING WITH NO LIMITATIONS

by Dr.Human for humanity on January 27, 2022.
© Dr. Hemendra Kumar Mandal, All rights reserved
As I am a poet I love
The art of writing to create sights and sounds
I like to sing with my heart's fairy wings
I like to fly towards the blue of sky and other things

I want to travel in all creative spheres
On the seas and I like to fly to the sky
I like to love romantically
With songs and smiles with rainbow colors

I want to meditate
and want to resonate
With my eternal soul
Till I reach my spiritual goal.......

SENSE OF THE SENSUAL LOVE

by Dr.Human for humanity on January 28, 2022.
© Dr. Hemendra Kumar Mandal, All rights reserved
He was full of virility and vigorous power
His strong arms encircled her
She wants to go up in his lap
Her sensuality wants his trap

At darkness of night
The both kissed light
With their warm hugs
They drowned into the sensual drugs

They don't see nothing other
They only drowned in the sea of love
The moments of the sands of time
Passed like a vanished star.....

POETRY IS THE LIFE OF A POET

by Dr.Human for humanity on January 28, 2022.
© Dr. Hemendra Kumar Mandal, All rights reserved

Why a poet writes a poem
Why men love women
Why we take tea
Why we go to sea

These queries have some abstract answers
Some have boomerang bouncers
Some say like God love His creations
So the poet love his preparations

His relaxation is his poem
His boundaries is his claim
His heaven is his joy
He can live on his poems convoy

On the colorful words and created musical voice
By his poems are his infallible choice.

MY ECSTATIC FLIGHT

by Dr.Human for humanity on January 28, 2022.
© Dr. Hemendra Kumar Mandal, All rights reserved
I am the lover of truth
I am the lover of faith
So I can kiss the death
Any time any day upto any breath

I want my ecstatic journey
To your Abode
O God let me enjoy easily
On your purity and colorful road

You can take me to your place
You can kiss me with grace
O God, O my lord
save me as I am bound with endless fraud

I want to bath in your fountain
I want your elixirs rain
I want to travel again and again
I want to be always in your cherished heaven.

I need the pure water of your blessings
On my head on my forehead forever

My heart sings
For you only and never for other

I cry I try to get your company
But I get only my useless enemy
Oh Jesus oh my father
Without your peace I will die rather

I cannot tolerate the eternal darkness
Beyond my residence
As I cherished your light
To come in all of my sight

Make me bold make me cool
Make me gold Make me only your tool
Make me the Rainbow on your abundant sky
Let me rest there let me meet your blissful high.

DUMB TONGUE IN SUCCUMBED SCENARIO

by Dr.Human for humanity on January 29, 2022.
© Dr. Hemendra Kumar Mandal, All rights reserved
Sometimes I can sing when the southern breeze blow
Sometimes My tired tummy don't want to go
Sometimes my tragic pain show
Become speechless by a moaning spirit's low

When the clouds of sad memories find it's way
When my brooding thoughts sway
My speech gets locked abruptly
And finds no way finally

When I feel lovelost
From my friends and lovers
I get speechless with no covers
At My heart and soul 's cost

When my self confidence touching the sky
But suddenly interrupted by my dear ones
I get broken from within with a great sigh
My speech gets disrupted at once.

MY MOM THE GREAT LOVE BOMB

by Dr.Human for humanity on January 31, 2022.
© Dr. Hemendra Kumar Mandal, All rights reserved
Love bursted from my mom
While raising my life as a good man
Her efforts were rewarding alone
As of now I Express her traits as I can

Now she is no more
Not here to grow more
Good traits and good faith
Into my blood to store

Her face with a smile
Was always in a rewarding style
Came to my heart
Her training was was lovable and smart

Oh God I can't express what I lost
She gave me love at her painstaking cost
After passing away only I realized her presence
My life is now imprisoned like a life sentence

She was my open air like cool sea breezes
She was my fountainhead of fairy tales
On her passing away I felt myself like a fist out of water
Now I can only remember her passionate care

I can't end my story about her
As her world was me her joy was my welfare
I can't assure whether she was goddess or human
My fountainhead of love was her life span

Now I became a beggar, a hopeless mind
As I am boundless with a mother's kind
My tears now dried but entered into my heart
Always tearing me with pains apart

A painstaking feeling into my sleep and dreams
Her absence chased me for long and made me scream
I could not imagine some day she will be no more
My world could be so colorless and bore

Oh God you don't know what you have done
By snatching my mother's love you have stunned
Me and my world of colors
In no time all are shunned.

COUNTRY GIRL IS MY PEARL

by Dr.Human for humanity on February 1, 2022.
© Dr. Hemendra Kumar Mandal, All rights reserved
You are my gemstone
Without you I am alone
You are so wild with forest smell
You are boundless lass like a strong male

You are muscular unlike city girl
The smell of soil is in your wall
The running vigour is in your veins
The horses run With you in the grass plains

You don't like artificial store of malls
As you have pretty village stalls
You are always with your wild frocks
And without the city girl's socks

You are gems in my eyes
Your dynamic life is full of spice
Your love and hate are all wild
Your kiss and hugs are cute and mild

Can you love me if I like you
As I like your life's careless view
Oh God give me gal of this type
Simplicity is whose watchword without any hype....

COW MILK WOW MILK!!!!!!

by Dr.Human for humanity on February 2, 2022.
© Dr. Hemendra Kumar Mandal, All rights reserved
Milk of cow
we don't know how
Give us nutritious food
Very nice healthy and good

They are so cool
They are farming tool
Of the agriculture of the country
They are our magical bounty

We get healthy and wealthy
By taking their elixirs produced free
They are worshipped in many countries
Due to their bestowed bliss in the form of Service

YOUR MAGICAL TOUCH WAS TO ME VERY MUCH ....

by Dr.Human for humanity on February 2, 2022.
© Dr. Hemendra Kumar Mandal, All rights reserved
May your love live long...
In my heart and soul may it throng
On the road by the beach
My memory is till now want there to reach

My first love got so much hype
That it was to my heart a golden type
Full of your gems and diamond rings
Brought to my eyes amazing dreams..

To our steps to the shore
Made our love depth more and more
By standing hand in hand
We thought our love was a valuable brand...

Sometimes I thought your pinkish kiss
Is came from a supernova with heavenly bliss
May God give our memories a long life
Through the centuries without any strife.....

TRANSCENDENTAL TRANSGENDER

by Dr.Human for humanity on February 2, 2022.
© Dr. Hemendra Kumar Mandal, All rights reserved
They are created at His will
They are bearing their wheel
They are alive by their force of will
But negligence of others is only pain they feel

Their confusion is not their creation
Their life still have some elegant motion
For this nobody should make any comment
All must accept their creator inflicted pains

GOLD IS GOLDEN THAT MAY EMBOLDEN

by Dr.Human for humanity on February 3, 2022.
© Dr. Hemendra Kumar Mandal, All rights reserved
The face value of your love power
Was not accepted due to your black colour
So mind was chasing some beautiful flower
May be or may not be sweet or sour

Your dress at first glance was not to impress
My light mind and You made me think with your face
You are so kind but it was wrong as I was blind
To see your soul to see your role in my mind

In the long run I could see your glittering face
Which is ugly but your soul was fresh
My heart my soul couldn't understand you
For which I had to repent and review.........

THE DANGEROUS SEA IS LIKE A BOUNDLESS BABY……

by Dr.Human for humanity on February 4, 2022.
© Dr. Hemendra Kumar Mandal, All rights reserved

Sea storm is the anger of the sea
On the Norwegian shore turning to me
Standing by the side trying to ride
at the top of tide…….

In an adventurous mood
A brave feeling is good
For me on the ship I can imagine
As if I am present there to witness the scene

Going to the shore
To view the uproar
The careless spontaneous beauty
Made me the dreamer of this fantasy

How did the painter feel
How his soul got drill
How his heart got the ecstatic thrill
When he painted the scenario with in his canvas which stood still.........

THE RUNNING BRIDE AGAINST THE TIDE .....

by Dr.Human for humanity on February 6, 2022.
© Dr. Hemendra Kumar Mandal, All rights reserved
The child was crying save me mummy
They will kill me with their enemy
She came running from her in laws
From her barbaric husband's paws

She was the victim of the pristine customs
Her future was being destroyed by thoughtless bordom
Mom save me either or God will not...

IN THE TEMPLE ON THE MOUNTAIN

by Dr.Human for humanity on February 6, 2022.
© Dr. Hemendra Kumar Mandal, All rights reserved
I found the caring mothers face
So nicely painted her lovely dress
I was compelled to pray her
I worship her with glittering flower

Prayed to love me to give me her compassion
To accompany me all my journeys against obsession
And life's odd endeavors
Help me to be free from evil force

I will sing for her in the prayers
Mother bless me and all and share
Your powerful blessing for all your children
who are tracing your love to wipe all stains..

AS A DOCTOR MY SERVICE TO A POOR CANCER PATIENT

by Dr.Human for humanity on February 8, 2022.
© Dr. Hemendra Kumar Mandal, All rights reserved
He was a very poor cancer patient
So he had no chance to find a doctor
So he was picked by an NGO where I was a member
I was a patron and admirer of their tent.

Once they called upon me to treat him
When I examined him I thought no doctor
Will be sufficient for him as it was his last stage so far
So I told my view to the organizers of the NGO team

They became upset but they we prepared for such blow
He had a tough kind of gum cancer
Always bleeding with ulcerative pus flow
He had no chance to survive so far as I know

Crying whole day long
with his pain that was very strong
I thought that death only can relieve his pains
My treatment had negligible palliative gains

Within a week or so
He was to bid adieu all the scenario
I was also very painful to see his pain
A thin black tall man can never maintain

The original health the original Joy of life
So it's on the hands of God to let him survive
Only unprecedented miracle on earth can regain
His Joy of life in his present reincarnation

I LOVED HER ONE WAY

by Dr.Human for humanity on February 8, 2022.
© Dr. Hemendra Kumar Mandal, All rights reserved
She was my fiance she was beautiful
She was God fearing and very cool
Thin with simple and white beauty
My life's nine years passed joyfully

She was always in a low key of her emotions
Her love was mixed with some fear without commotion
But at last she informed me of her breast cancer
I was too upset to find any answer...

A veil of darkness a shot of depression
Made me hopeless with painful emotion
I had no choice or any voice to counter this
I was afraid to love her but couldn't dismiss

One day she came to me with an offer
If you don't marry me I have to marry another
Her face was cool as before
I couldn't advance anymore

Over my silence
She was depressed
But even with my pure love
To conquer my selfishness was too tough.

SENSUALITY OF SENSITIVE SEX

by Dr.Human for humanity on February 9, 2022.
© Dr. Hemendra Kumar Mandal, All rights reserved

I have seen in the park
everywhere in the dark
In the school and in the bathroom of trains
the sex juice vigorously drains

Notwithstanding any ethical values
Promiscuity among young let loose
They believe in one night stands
Just enjoy their own sexual brands

All forms of sex are used to satisfy themselves
No strings bound in their figures always
While spilling lubricants along the dresses
Jeans are much wet with semen and juices

They are mad while enjoying each other
They never think of ethics as those they don't bother
But when those acts are over
They think for a while what was hovering over....

On the other there is a sea of unwed mothers
They just fell in a dilemma between life and death
What to do or not to as they are short of breath
Depression at this age are on the rampage......

POETIC SUBLIMATION FOR ULTIMATE CIVILIZATION

by Dr.Human for humanity on February 9, 2022.
© Dr. Hemendra Kumar Mandal, All rights reserved
Poet is not a normal being
Made up of common thing
Of anger of desire,
With an unusual desire

He is taller than normal beings
He always maintains high mood and sings
The songs of equality
Always sings for humanity

He must dream weird dreams
To give ultimate freedom to human beings
So he is never a normal man to enjoy
Common things which are not with his convoy

He has enough depth to enter into that heaven
His thought power takes him to all uneven
Things of joy he is love He is romantic even
He makes his own gateway to the immortal heaven.

THE FAIRNESS OF THE FAIRY

by Dr.Human for humanity on February 9, 2022.
© Dr. Hemendra Kumar Mandal, All rights reserved
You can tell a fairly tale
You can go through
forests and seas with ringing bell
It is not cumbersome and tough

The depth of forest invites uninvited guests
Their unusual dances and songs tests
Their beautiful lovely attire
The fairy is at their center

Their days are passed with all sunshine
Their joy consists of nothing but gruff voice singing
Their uninvited dance makes the great forest show
All animals are united to greet their fairy's show

The sun and also the moon
Became astonished very soon
By their nice and unique get together
Which nobody seen till now and will see never.....

YOU ARE MY LOVE TEACHER

by Dr.Human for humanity on February 9, 2022.
© Dr. Hemendra Kumar Mandal, All rights reserved

May be the jesus is love preacher
But you are my love teacher
When I only was sensible enough to love you
You had only changed my adulterated view

When the moon was rising on the eastern sky
At first I was shy
Shy to get into your freedom
Shy to make you my woman

But you trained me to that balance
Of body and soul
In a mature nature so cool
I admired your this stance

When your emotions were flying high
You loved me with a romantic sigh
When you were brand new to my eyes
Your smiling beauty had a magnetic price

You drawn me towards your magic
I became hypnotized and sick
For your attractive life
At last after a long drive you became my wife..

THE LIGHTS OF DARKNESS

by Dr.Human for humanity on February 9, 2022.
© Dr. Hemendra Kumar Mandal, All rights reserved
Now the sun is no more
The mesmerizing darkness soar
To an amazing height
The hearts opened somewhere very bright

The people who not found food in the daylight
Thought this time for them is alright
The lovers who were shy at daylight
Finds freedom to get their sexual right

The nocturnal people and animals
Find their time to get their trials
For the demands of their hidden souls
For their natural as well as unnatural goals

THE ALIENS

by Dr.Human for humanity on February 10, 2022.
© Dr. Hemendra Kumar Mandal, All rights reserved
They are extraordinary and extraterrestrial
Being curious about our civilization which is abnormal
To them and their people
They want to inform us on their riddle

And bu turn They want to mix up with us
But they have enough fear and curious
How we shall accept them in their omnibus
In their planet or in their stars from where they came to us

Their innumerable indications to our people
Their scores of transportation are capable
Enough to round about the globe in no time
They always poke their nose like lovers vibe

They want to mingle with this planet
But both of us are not yet set
To transfer our technology and diplomatic tie
To exchange the intelligence which are sky high

Their figures are different from the different planets
As they come, they are too peculiar to get set
In this environment as they always radiate
Extraterrestrial radiation foreign to our environment

THE TICKING ON THE SANDS OF TIME

by Dr.Human for humanity on February 10, 2022.
© Dr. Hemendra Kumar Mandal, All rights reserved
At the dead of night silence is reigning
But time is ticking without resting
Like all day on all the way
As an immortal being

It don't care the pleasure and pain
It never allows to happen same thing again
The controller of the other two factors space and person
It oversees equally peace murders or arson

The death is its servant as well as the newborn
The boundless sea and the sky above may be stubborn
But all are compelled to obey it's dictates
Be it living or non living all must follow it's fate.

YOU CHASED ME THROUGHOUT MY LIFE

by Dr.Human for humanity on February 12, 2022.
© Dr. Hemendra Kumar Mandal, All rights reserved
Thy name is sex full of virility
nudity and beauty, ohh you are my cutie
My black and white life got many strife
But I couldn't shun you and your fleshy life

I am a common man but that doesn't meant
I haven't any desire for your juicy lips which didn't
Attract my juices to your colorful ones
From the days of my youth you called me with trance

When I see your incarnations in the sea Beaches
Roads Highways half nude half clad with inviting speeches
I can't but go my parents my girlfriends teaches
But still your naughty eye lashes preaches

Come to me my sweetheart just try to know
Who am I just like a meteorite blow
To your deserted heart came with juices flow
Till you reach Your heaven with my magic show...

YOU MUST KNOW POWER CORRUPTS .....

by Dr.Human for humanity on February 12, 2022.
© Dr. Hemendra Kumar Mandal, All rights reserved
Yes my red brothers or black ones
From the Darwins propositions
You better know the harsh truth
Even you experienced through

Your lives of tortures by the whites
But still they are not civilized even after fights
They couldn't be able to confer your rights
To live with freedom with peaceful sleeps of nights

Selfishness is a word which make men fools
They have brains but no intelligent tools
To think clear, to think liberal for all
In the same spirits without any downfall.

MY DANCING ONLY FOR YOU

by Dr.Human for humanity on February 12, 2022.
© Dr. Hemendra Kumar Mandal, All rights reserved
Like peacocks, or the parrots or sea gulls love
My dance is only for you with all colorful stuff
I don't know why but my mind becomes high
Without any apparent cause it begins to fly..

Is it love Is it beauty or is it a compassion for you
But I don't know why I forget all by your single view
My body or soul I try to find where is you
But didn't find any space of my presence without you

Am I became mad or very sad with all the world
Where you don't go or don't throw your word
All colors all flowers and birds reminds me
You are my blood flow through my veins with glee.

THE DARKNESS PREVAILS BUT ....

by Dr.Human for humanity on February 13, 2022.
© Dr. Hemendra Kumar Mandal, All rights reserved
The night is coming second by seconds
Minute by minute as the darkness bonds
With the sea with the deserts and sky view
But the people of the forest and animals knew

It time for their play for quarrel and games
With their closed relationships and friends
The sounds of their anger come from very far
Like the beauty of many kinds of whispers

The moonshine made the magical view
The earth is getting amazing look very new
The tired employees are returning from their jobs
For their children wives so beautiful heartthrobs

THE FEAST BY YOUR BEAUTY.....

by Dr.Human for humanity on February 14, 2022.
© Dr. Hemendra Kumar Mandal, All rights reserved
I was like a light bug of the city
Came running to your beauty
Which was the light of your body
Made me magnetic to you and so moody...

The moon was on the sky
Below was snowy evening
My thrills came like a shooting
And made me your crazy guy

As the morning became very mistic
Your body with a thin boutique
Creating amazing showdown
Attracted my whole attention to your slipping gown

The glittering polish of your skin
Was like my fantasy of you in dreams
Which made me forget the surrounding
Only you were my sole target and all are missing

LOVE IS AMAZING

by Dr.Human for humanity on February 14, 2022.
© Dr. Hemendra Kumar Mandal, All rights reserved
Love floats on the sea
Of my feelings of the boundless me
My petals like a rose
Spreads perfume and glows

By your touch made of heaven
By your body and soul
With great energy driven
Meets our pleasure goal

MY POEM MY DREAMS MY LOVE'S CHOCOLATE CREAMS

by Dr.Human for humanity on February 15, 2022.
© Dr. Hemendra Kumar Mandal, All rights reserved

My poems are my inspiration to live long
My nature my beauty of heart go along
With the color and essence of words
That inspires me and my worlds

I start singing on my poems beauty
And get much enjoyment so naturally
That I need nobody to play with me
I can travel to the height of scented beauty

My love also comes to me on this way
Like the springtime chenar sway
With a dancing mood from parlour
Vigorous virile that is my harbor

Waiting for me my fiance
With her wide eyes come to me
To see my face with jealousy
If I am still is her somebody

PROGRAMED FOR A PURPOSE

by Dr.Human for humanity on February 15, 2022.
© Dr. Hemendra Kumar Mandal, All rights reserved
There is a proverb that whom God love die young
Actually God love His cherished son and long
For their return to His abode
He measured their road

They travel along the direction of His direction
They have no freedom as God directs their motion
HIS coveted disciples are not free to live here
As He is only their controller

They are the security guards of His kingdom
So they have particular duties for their stardom

LOVE THE GREATNESS OF GOODNESS

by Dr.Human for humanity on February 20, 2022.
© Dr. Hemendra Kumar Mandal, All rights reserved
I can reach the mountain high for love
I can reach the blue firmament above
For your love I can dive into the deep sea
As my love for you makes me free

My love is a beautiful dish made up of your feelings
I can mix many colors with your endless dealings
I can paint your face always smiling
I must accompany always your lovely walking

MOST COMPLEX WORK IS TO BE SIMPLE

by Dr.Human for humanity on February 21, 2022.
© Dr. Hemendra Kumar Mandal, All rights reserved
Simplicity is the cherished goal of all
But it is not the cup of tea of all
The lovely behavior comes with the blessings
Of the great God who is tracing the missing

Sons of quality of goodness and greatness
We try to be his lovely children
But we go astray from our aim
So we don't get our cherished place

The simple person never gets depressed
Whatever are the problems to be accessed

Author notes
74 words

THE ADVENT OF A MAN OF 70

by Dr.Human for humanity on February 21, 2022.
© Dr. Hemendra Kumar Mandal, All rights reserved
I think of you how much pleasure and pain
You faced in this life again and again
So that your faith on life and God
Somewhat decreased on the lord

The fighting in your daily life was full of struggle and strife
But still you always managed to survive
From this cycle of pleasure and pain
So that your experience goes not in vain

Love hate Joy and woe all are the living show
In the theater of the world of plenty
Where we try to invent our lifestyle flow
At the end of its existence we face the cruelty

EVERY SINNER HAS A FUTURE EVERY SAINT HAD A PAST

by Dr.Human for humanity on February 22, 2022.
© Dr. Hemendra Kumar Mandal, All rights reserved
Yes I do believe in that
The sinners must shun lust
The saint must shower blessings
As the world wants his preaching

God bless those who has arisen
From their hibernation again and again
By the internal war with negative sense
As they are their life's essence

Can we grow without the irrigation by goodness
Without His eternal and powerful witness
The money the greed are all temporary and evil
So we need to go along the path of HIS will

We don't take fresh air for breathing
As we are always losing the good health
The pure love pure thoughts from heaven
Are lacking and we are losing our hard earned wealth.

ROLE OF THE OPPRESSED AND OPPRESSORS

by Dr.Human for humanity on February 22, 2022.
© Dr. Hemendra Kumar Mandal, All rights reserved
When both are the sides of the same coin
It is just the play of times which take stain
And gets the roles in turn without any reasoning
The ego comes and goes and makes our ruining

The moon at night becomes the sun at the day
As humans are too weak to assert their way
Weak needs laws but strong finds flaws in that
To get all selfish ends to destroy goodness fast

Sometimes clouds has audacity to cover the sun
But at another time they are easily gone
But when it begins to rain darkness comes
Sun and moon both become deafs and dumbs.

WORD IS OMNIPOTENT

by Dr.Human for humanity on February 22, 2022.
© Dr. Hemendra Kumar Mandal, All rights reserved

The utterance of the good or bad
Has its inherent beauty sometimes very sad
Depends on the personality
And the equality and adversity

If you have the power
Then it can shower
The tune of beauty
But if you are too weak to perform the duty

Then nothing will save you from destruction
As you have no ideas of construction
You may preach truth or falsehood
Then you may get into the history for good

The history repeated again and again
Around this adage of good and evil
Sometimes they are born to kill
Sometimes they are used in vain.

ADDICTION WHEN IT IS A DICTION

by Dr.Human for humanity on February 23, 2022.
© Dr. Hemendra Kumar Mandal, All rights reserved
Addiction is the disease of the youth nowadays
This generation is going to their destructive ways
To escape from the struggle of life
For avoiding unavoidable strife

They are getting sick by the pressure of career
The pressure of the parent and near and dear
They are forced to a level they cannot reach
But still their friends and family teach

Which they are unable to do
As everyone has a limit that is true
They may be encouraged
But to their utter dismay they are derailed

THE HINGLISH LANGUAGE

by Dr.Human for humanity on February 25, 2022.
© Dr. Hemendra Kumar Mandal, All rights reserved
The colloquial uses of English with punch of Hindi
Is called here as Hinglish it's a peculiar modus operandi
Of the users weak in the use of a foreign language
As it is very tough to them to assimilate it's usage

In other vernacular also English is punched
In a peculiar phonetics and launched
To use it as a makeshift language
For the daily life feasibility and its usage

The Hindi and English punched to pronounce Hinglish
Which are used by many Indian states while using English
In a faulty way but they has no other alternative
As in their daily life after all they have to survive

IMPRISONED IN THE TRAP OF HIS OWN

by Dr.Human for humanity on February 25, 2022.
© Dr. Hemendra Kumar Mandal, All rights reserved
We are walking always on the razors blades
In this unpredictable world of our own shades
We make blunders in our love or romance or careers
Which makes us repent and give us fears

Which may even endanger our lives
Which makes us roar or Which leads to cries
We then take resort of wrong roads or lies
Getting trapped and it becomes difficult to survive

Our parents and relatives are also trapped
In an awkward situation which they never shaped
Also in their lives never ever imagined
One bolt from the blue destroyed everything aligned

REINCARNATION IS A FACT NOT IMAGINATION

by Dr.Human for humanity on February 25, 2022.
© Dr. Hemendra Kumar Mandal, All rights reserved
If I am to born again I will not cram facts like parrot and
become a bookish animal rather I will train my mind for
concentration and meditation and with that invincible
mind I will aquire facts if need be there at all.......
SWAMI VIVEKANANDA

Mind is a powerful tool given by our creator
If we have a strong mind we will be salvaged forever
Reincarnation is not a joke or imagination
Certified by Almost all God's own statesman

In the next Reincarnation we should streamline us
In a new environment of our own and change the status
Of this birth towards the God and salvation
I must always pray to leave these worldly competitions

The fruits of human life is for distribution
Who deserve these for their own salvation
As the great came this foreign world to take them above
The petty thoughts and irrigate their minds with the
elixirs of sheer love.

I COULD NOT IMAGINE THAT DAY WILL EVER COME

by Dr.Human for humanity on February 27, 2022.
© Dr. Hemendra Kumar Mandal, All rights reserved

The day of death of my mom was a nightmare to me
Even in my worst dreams I couldn't imagine it will be
Such a great disaster in my life as I couldn't imagine
All on a sudden it came without any notice even

I was on a job 40 kilometers away and stayed there
I used to see her by bike when I found time for her
But she was old but not so feeble
So I couldn't think the death will so horrible

And snatch her from me just after two days
When I returned to my job place
But when that ominous day came
I murmured oh God I couldn't see her last it's very shame

At one word or two could quench my thirst
Remembered the day I had seen her first
Then as life rolled on she was was very concerned
Over my well being and a good payment is earned

She always talked to me till the end
How to lead a good life and problems to mend
I still remember her cool eyes full of affection
When looked at me on my life life's any tension.

Ohh God bless her soul wherever she is
As she was my only friend philosopher and guide
All the way of my life till her end
Ohh God peace will prevail, mom like humans if you can send…

WHEN PASSION IS COMPASSIONATE

by Dr.Human for humanity on March 1, 2022.
© Dr. Hemendra Kumar Mandal, All rights reserved
We are created by the almighty
For the love of each other rightly
But we couldn't understand his dictate
And don't think that way and go against

The animals also hungry of love affection
If you can give it they will always maintain
Your safety and peace and give their best
And help to increase your joy and pass all your tests

They gradually become your family member
And with their sixth sense they will love you forever
God also becomes pleased by your feelings
He will love you in all HIS dealings

Author notes
93 words

THE SCORN IS BORN WITHOUT ANY MOTHER AND ANY NORM

by Dr.Human for humanity on March 3, 2022.
© Dr. Hemendra Kumar Mandal, All rights reserved
Really we prove ourselves foolish
When we scorn others bullish
We try to show off us as intelligent as anything
But lastly it is proven useless in the ring

Sometimes we support wars as justified
When our men are vehemently deprived
But in other case we hanker for peace
As we came from heaven to share God's grace

So naturally people laugh at us
As our comments proved to be farce
We are always showing off our selfishness
And those fools are praying for God's grace

They are enemies of our civilization
They are the war mongers of any nation
They never seen the mothers tears
They never felt the soldiers fears

They are blind to spilling blood in the war fronts
They are heartless except their dear ones
So they have no right to survive
One day they will turn into an extinct tribe.....

HUNGRY AND THE OLD MAN

by Dr.Human for humanity on March 8, 2022.
© Dr. Hemendra Kumar Mandal, All rights reserved

Hungry has nothing to eat
While the rich old man has every sweet treat
But still they both are thin skinny lifeless
They always feeling loss of energy and useless

The Hungry is universal in poverty
But the old man feeling his age's anxiety
Hungry is too weak to walk
Likewise the old is diseased to talk

The peculiar creation of God is so tactful
He made both poor and rich equivalent needful
To think over it I became amazed
What a miraculous earth HE created!!!

THE GIGGLING BABY

by Dr.Human for humanity on March 8, 2022.
© Dr. Hemendra Kumar Mandal, All rights reserved
Her little sensations are overwhelming
Her father was sitting in the temple
But she wanted running
When she came to him so simple

He whispered to her don't shout don't run
He got her seated beside him
Still she was giggling as best as she can
To her every movement was like a dream

Her father was her companion
Like a playfull instrument
She wanted always to enjoy the motion
Her every feelings are hell bent.

KIDS LOVE DYNAMICS

by Dr.Human for humanity on March 8, 2022.
© Dr. Hemendra Kumar Mandal, All rights reserved

The baby boy was sitting in the temple with his mother
Suddenly some people beside him moved to leave further
All on a sudden the baby boy went with them leaving his mom
After a while she discovered that he moved alone

The baby boy of two years liked the movement
Rather seating still at a place with an attachment
Such is the psychology of the baby
He is only attached to the motion that's steady

He knows no relation mom or dad
Except dynamic scenario everything is bad
To him as he is born to play
He is the son of pleasure wants to enjoy all the way.

I HAVE GOT YOU AT LAST....

by Dr.Human for humanity on March 14, 2022.
© Dr. Hemendra Kumar Mandal, All rights reserved
Our love was not too fast
We have seen each other near past
Then I remembered your beautiful memory
No expected you to come my way So fiery

Days gone by my casual life had no upheaval
But suddenly once again you came like a carnival
Our common friend Alfred introduced us
And then our hot bodies made occasional touch

By the shake of hands or kiss of lips
We both got the introductory love tips
Then we wandered under the sun and moon
To find our cozy bedroom full of elixirs spoon

You signed me to come close
The day you invited me with bountiful rose
We were alone that day no one to disturb under the moon
We found our resonating life very hot very soon

POETS' ROLE IN THESE TOUGH TIMES

by Dr.Human for humanity on March 14, 2022.
© Dr. Hemendra Kumar Mandal, All rights reserved
Wars are abundant and overwhelming
Peace is fearful and bleeding
The newborns the children of God crying
But nobody is there to take care of their dying

Under the missiles as not the needs of babies
Prioritized but the demons hungers are satisfied
Not the flowers essence and colors got views
But the missiles hues replaced the western skies

The hospitals schools of the children demolished
The wars don't care why the mothers bred child
Why the lovers drew near to flourish civilization
The wars only knows the technology of destruction

So you the poet take some rest now
As your pen is bleeding by the bullets row
The sun moon the green and blue
Replaced only by the ashes of the dark hue

Don't go out dear poet
humanity is now forgotten your flavor
As he has no time of creation
As he is is busy in destruction

If any day comes
if anything survived by the balms
Then you may have access to the new
The again your hearts will get new worlds
view..............

Now is panic everyday everywhere
The death trailers are here and there
The bodies of the great soldiers the victim of the war
Went to a hell of meaningless show of power......

WAITING FOR THE DAY

by Dr.Human for humanity on March 16, 2022.
© Dr. Hemendra Kumar Mandal, All rights reserved
I am now disgusted of the wars
As a poet waiting for the day
When the soldiers will hate to see blood
Of their and compatriots innocent bleeding families

And decide to throw away the uniforms
Which takes away the blood of humans
On which the political leaders will be hopeless
To maintain their armies and the war fortress

The destruction of economy will also be for long
Which earned by The blood and toils of their near and dear ones...
The hunger will reign for years to come
As this little common sense of the political leaders
WILL NEVER COME.....

I KNOW BUT MAYBE YOU DON'T

by Dr.Human for humanity on March 18, 2022.
© Dr. Hemendra Kumar Mandal, All rights reserved
The place is colorless dark
Except the red umbrella showing its hue
As a promise to protect from torrential rain back
And the promise to the lives to renew

Nobody is there in a lonely street
Probably nobody liked it
Even the animals lizards cockroaches got it
As they don't want to soak in the rain and fight

The history of Paris was silently repeating
Through day and night
With colorful days and colorless nights dreams
Like centuries before it has got the same sight

It has now and then prepared the theater
Of the new environment of struggle so far
Love for lovers war for fighter
Art for artists and dreams for the dreamers....

HAPPINESS IS INBORN NOT ARTIFICIALLY MADE

by Dr.Human for humanity on March 20, 2022.
© Dr. Hemendra Kumar Mandal, All rights reserved
Like the leadership in you is inborn
The happiness is also like a beautiful son
Who comes to please a family all the way
Like a beautiful flower through the breezes sway

We know happiness is a glow imminent
Exudes from a beautiful character innocent
Like a carefree wind in the springs
Like a rainbow color in our dreams

Happiness is the first meeting with my love
Till the fading away of it over and above
The new waves coming on the way
Again and again it's juices in my mind got its spray

Happiness is the view of a moon in a lonely sky
Comes With the magic of glittering moonshine very high
When to enjoy it I was alone but not sad
Because my happiness never ever got my feelings bad

WORLD POETRY DAY 21ST MARCH DEDICATED TO LONG MARCH FOR POETS

by Dr.Human for humanity on March 21, 2022.
© Dr. Hemendra Kumar Mandal, All rights reserved
Today is the day remembered for the poets
Today is the day dedicated to the blood toil and sweats
Of the common man, of the uncommon man
Who can enjoy the poems and then can scan

Those garden of beautiful flowers
Beautiful genres of lovers
Those creations not less than those of God's
Which can only be dedicated with purity to the lords

Which calls for peace
But unheeded by the selfish
Which grows the elixirs
From the heart we miss

They cry for others
They cry for brothers
Wherever they live
May They always survive

The wars the fires the bombs
Sending them to their tombs
Their mothers cry with the bleeding hearts
As once they alighted through their cozy wombs...

NO WAR CAN BE FOUGHT WITHOUT LOVE

by Dr.Human for humanity on March 22, 2022.
© Dr. Hemendra Kumar Mandal, All rights reserved
The war itself is begging for survival from near and dears
To the love from its mother brother and family members
When they come from their destruction mentality
They need at first is love from their family beauty

They want to enjoy the life at one ground
And destroy it at another tragic point around
So my dear friends The war is like a Satan gone astray
It can never survive if you don't pamper it anyway

It's the collision head on through your ego
It's the brutal play sometimes for which we go
Just for the flexing of our muscles to show
Then at last Our power and pomp and position we know......

For war we need food and shelter
Which is grown with blood and toils of farmer
We need technology for destruction
Which is made by scientists meditation

Then without peacetime preparation
Wars have no base no position
Like sometimes we cry we bleed
Just by our own made accidents indeed.....

THE WOMAN MEANS THE WHOLE OF CIVILIZATION

by Dr.Human for humanity on March 22, 2022.
© Dr. Hemendra Kumar Mandal, All rights reserved
There is no scope to overemphasize
As woman is only the heart to mesmerize
The civilization, the energy behind every motion
Of this planet in all the spheres in all its commotion

From the cradle to grave women are all in all
The mother in her awaken when her baby crawls
The leader the teacher the fighter in all her roles
She is confident enough to reach her goals

She controls the men with love and joy
She maintains the family with her convoy
Her pleasure and pains her strength and weakness
leads her family with thick and thin always

Her responsibilities are beyond measures
As she is always pregnant with invaluable treasures
Her in born talents always mends the bleeding earth
As she is the mother of all children from their birth...

Author notes

133 words

THE THREE DEATHS IN A BIKE ACCIDENT

by Dr.Human for humanity on March 26, 2022.
© Dr. Hemendra Kumar Mandal, All rights reserved
The news was rolling on
All on a sudden my nerves were electrified
As my vision fall on the lying dead bodies
They were young and strong vibrant bodies

As a poet I became cold for sometime
Thinking a lot about their abruptly ended lives
Their destroyed future within a seconds notice
Their lives and souls flew to the unknown and vanished.

Like other cases at the time of their surmise
Nobody was there to greet them to their destination
No parents no families came happened all on a sudden
Do their bodies want to say something?
To this mortal world
Don't do plans to go here and there
As you are not going through your own plans either!!!

DYNAMICS OF LIFE IS BROUGHT BY WAR......

by Dr.Human for humanity on March 30, 2022.
© Dr. Hemendra Kumar Mandal, All rights reserved

War to snatch bread from you
War for seating by window for better view
War for tasty foods
War for traveling to country woods

So it depends on what do you mean
By the War which always remain
Just at your side in the family
In the school shooting fiercely

War for diseases within
War for sex desire cooling
It may amount to murder
To snatch your baby from her lover

War amounts to go for an ego
So only for this you throw your blow
If blood doesn't run for War
Your lives are standstill and reach nowhere

The sisters make War for the same lover
Results may be suicide or murder
So wars have no clear cause to go for
As humans behave like Mads and walks with armor

The heats of War are within their blood
So it is reflected everyday like flood
In the parties and casinos
Adrenalin always haphazardly goes

To an unknown journey
To take adventurous foray
War between parents amount to divorce
Shattering the lives of the children and force

To the hunger and uncertainty of future
Simply by the useless egoism and War
Sometimes I think we are prone to this
Our defects from the birth is The cause of all the evils.

WARS ARE PLAY FOR LEADERS AS THEY AREN'T SUFFERERS

by Dr.Human for humanity on March 30, 2022.
© Dr. Hemendra Kumar Mandal, All rights reserved
War is never an intelligent option
Both parties are fool with wrong emotions
They are irresponsible leaders
They are anger breeders

Both Moscow and Kiev are fools
As they lost their hard earned cools
From some trifling war of ego's
Many lives they lose

Which are not their own
The lives are of people who are unknown
Who has nothing to do with daily life
Nothing to think over political strife

Both Putin and Jelensky both are fools
They never know the wars rules
They should be shoot at sight
To understand the innocents plight

Putin is fool but jelensky is more
From the intimacy to Nato he made useless uproar
Nato never came to rescue
Foolish Jelensky never knew

And destroyed innocent lives and property
Of his country pushing it to eternal poverty
Nothing was his gain
The history will never seen Foolish leader like him again………

AMBITIOUS HUMANS MADE THEMSELVES ROBOTS

by Dr.Human for humanity on March 31, 2022.
© Dr. Hemendra Kumar Mandal, All rights reserved
We are nowadays busy for nothing
We are not pleased even we have everything
Because we made Graves of our feelings
Long before our physical death and ending

We say thanks without any exchange of joy
We are running not physically but with mechanical convoy
We make love marriage with Loveless calculations
As a means of making money formulation

We forget to laugh with friends and families
Busy enough to accept robotic mechanics
We became more of machines than humans
We are placed in railway tracks like wagons

Even with girlfriends wives and every relationships
We think of money making and profits
So pleasure of relationships fled to a sky high
And we are compelled to say them GOODBYE.....

DAYDREAMING....
PROMPT..1

by Dr.Human for humanity on April 1, 2022.
© Dr. Hemendra Kumar Mandal, All rights reserved
Apart from my night dreams and nightmares
I loved to do daydreaming without cares
Remembering my childhood days
I used to be precocious always

I ran with the Butterflies in the greenfield
I dreamed my next plan to be built
On which platter and to do it better
With the surprise of my friends shelter

To their own character of building
On the sands beside the sea dancing
All the day running and running till their angry moms
Fixed their playing norms without any mercy terms

Sometimes in the closet of a room and wait
I used to sit for hours planning what to do next
I called for my friends to their surprise
New discoveries which were unconventional and very nice.

Author notes
Prompt one

WHEN I WAS JUST A CURIOUS BOY OF 8 YEARS

by Dr.Human for humanity on April 1, 2022.
© Dr. Hemendra Kumar Mandal, All rights reserved

I had a friend of same age
We found both a meditation stage
By a water body with green pasture
We tried to meditate there

Like a hermit on the Himalayas
As someone related about the pious
Residing on the mountains
And they are very powerful with magical moments

I was amazed with those stories
So I discussed the same without worries
With my only precocious friend of that time
We wanted some feelings which were sublime

We went there regularly
After or before our school times minutely
As we imagined those stories of the sages
Who are extraordinary in their own life stages....

FACELESS FACIAL

by Dr.Human for humanity on April 2, 2022.
© Dr. Hemendra Kumar Mandal, All rights reserved
The colour in me was fading
As depression was growing
My life was drowning in the sea
My life colors was fading and leaving me

Promises by lover were sky high
But at last all were in vain and dry.

Author notes

40 words

BLEEDING HEARTS

by Dr.Human for humanity on April 3, 2022.
© Dr. Hemendra Kumar Mandal, All rights reserved

The hearts are bleeding
But why oh God keep me reeling
Under your advice keep me cool
As I am not brave enough to rule

The hearts of me as well as others
I cannot control the infections came from Travellers
So give me strength to fight
In those directions which are right

The depressions are engulfing our little green planet
Wake up call is ringing please don't get upset
The frustrated ambitions are producing the heat
The ghosts are running to the humans to greet

So invent the proper vaccine to survive
From the abruptly attacking infectious drive
Otherwise the hearts will bleed
The love for our fellows will vanish indeed.

DELUGE THE EARTH BY YOUR MIRTH

by Dr.Human for humanity on April 3, 2022.
© Dr. Hemendra Kumar Mandal, All rights reserved
Be positive do positive
Which in turn will give
Always Joy to your living vibration
With a dynamic and ecstatic motion

The role of negative thoughts
Always contorts
Our way of thinking towards a desert
Of dry and devoid of water going smart

The blow of the storm and breeze
Instantly freshen our our mind and seize
The darkness without light
That removes the regular stains of fight

Our lives need the deluge of joy
Otherwise it will always annoy
The truth behind the humanity
The optimism takes us to infinity

Of our own inner joy of sublimation
Which transports to progression of our nation
No war no distraction from the truth
Can only entertain our soul now going with untruths.

Storms and darkness will always come our way
But positive thinker don't care all those and don't sway
Buy these evil forces as he has the armor which endorsed
His power of creative joy with his own rules enforced....

MY HEART IS BROKEN INSIDE

by Dr.Human for humanity on April 3, 2022.
© Dr. Hemendra Kumar Mandal, All rights reserved
I talk laugh enjoy your company my dear friend
But It doesn't reveal my bleeding heart's cruel end
I keep my frustration and depression from all
But sometimes I fail to suppress the incessant fall

Which are getting worse day by day
Which I can't not control in any way
My picture is perfect beyond doubt
But at the dead end of night I have to shout

Oh God save me from the danger created by my own
Give me the pleasure of your truth which are shown
In your scriptures in you sweet dreams and word
As without you my heart's darkness always bombard

Nowhere to go nowhere to show my heat of heart
Which at one hand bleeding and at other hand
trying to be smart
Really it's a pseudo nature of my mind
Oh God save me from this darkness and be kind.......

IF WINTER COMES CAN SPRING BE FAR BEHIND ?... OSCAR WILDE

by Dr.Human for humanity on April 4, 2022.
© Dr. Hemendra Kumar Mandal, All rights reserved
Yes winter is in its full bloom
But the sparrow don't know as it has no room
For resting in a cozy environment
It has to struggle for its immediate refreshment

For its own and immediate newborn family
She is responsible enough to take of them naturally.

Author notes
6 lines

MY FUTURE....

by Dr.Human for humanity on April 4, 2022.
© Dr. Hemendra Kumar Mandal, All rights reserved

I had many attractive plans in the past
To construct my life with amazing start
I wanted to be einstein at first
But he also disenchanted with this human lust

He was disgusted with the so called civilization
Too much sophisticated but all in vain
So he declared his future in Reincarnation
As a simple farmer if he is to be born again

So I changed my plan for being a Spiritual aspirant
Which teaches humans to be simple and adamant
Like the Jesus or else who are innocent but interesting
And all love him as a best God head human being.

BEAUTY IS SKIN DEEP

by Dr.Human for humanity on April 4, 2022.
© Dr. Hemendra Kumar Mandal, All rights reserved
Beauty lies in the beholder's eye
It is not dependent on its imperfections however it's high
Beauty of the rose with thorns is more beautiful
Than without it as it is dependent on the viewer's cool

So also in a love affairs Beauty is a combo offer
With the offer of body and soul of the lovers
The beauty of her eyes is cool and nice
It glues the hearts in an exceptional heights

The concept of ugliness is also dependent on the viewer's discretion
Your ugly body sometimes covered by souls attention
So in China the little foot of girls are beautiful
But in other country it very ugly and never it's cool

So rose beauty depends on my view of it's qualities also
The pricking of it's thorn is then a secondary show
The night is not beautiful but when moon comes
It makes the time entertaining and a heavenly entrance

APRIL'S FULL ENTERTAINMENT

by Dr.Human for humanity on April 4, 2022.
© Dr. Hemendra Kumar Mandal, All rights reserved
The month has came with different colors
Of the sweet breeze and vibrant flowers
The children and the old equally enjoy
The beautiful nature's amazing convoy

The animals flowers people and showers
From the nature's powers
Came with eternal variety
God also came this month with his ingenuity.

A NAUGHTY GIRL

by Dr.Human for humanity on April 4, 2022.
© Dr. Hemendra Kumar Mandal, All rights reserved

I met a naughty girl very bold
Smiling on my way unprovoked
Her dress was inviting
To my naughty senses chuckling

She was full of gestures without any word
When followed she tried to bombard
To my man force but I was shy
At the street corner her virility became high

She stopped for a while there
Meanwhile I was also curious to stare
Her beautiful attractive assets
Made me follow her without any mess

Her invitation was clear but without any word
So I was a bit shy to go forward
To attract her in an open relationship
Then her smile unhindered tried to give

The final signal to her residence
In a dinghy dark room having no sense
Of joy and happiness as it's her business
She was a whore whose profession is not goodness.

THE ORDEAL WAS WHERE I WAS THE WITNESS, THE CANCER

by Dr.Human for humanity on April 5, 2022.
© Dr. Hemendra Kumar Mandal, All rights reserved

I was living in rent to my landlords house
The husband wife lived there without any issues
Their lives were monotonous without any children
But one day cancer came to greet them

The wife old at about 60 years
Diseased with the cancer
Her health degraded day by day
Treatments were in vain deteriorating every way

At first the husband a real good man
Borne all pains as he can
But there was a limit to it
He was exhausted by the hopeless outfit

She became very sick and thin every day
A governess kept came out to be a thief one day
Due to the pain and exhaustion of the disease
She could not eat anything in her last days at ease

The exhausted husband abused her sometimes
As he couldn't bear the pain anymore in front of him
Living in the same room side by side
Something he thought even for a suicide

The doctors at first admitted for a few days
Lastly they suggested to keep the patient at home
as there was no hope rays
One day at the end of limitless exhaustion she gave up fight for life
Ending everything and death wiper her all strife

After all rituals as per hindu cemetery rules
The last right done with all the tools
Once a life came on this mother earth
On another day it was deleted as dead from her registration of birth......

THE FALLING WATER FROM WATERFALLS

by Dr.Human for humanity on April 5, 2022.
© Dr. Hemendra Kumar Mandal, All rights reserved
The water has no rest from the time immemorial
It is falling falling and falling with its intentions real
The blue sky is gazing in ita meditative mood
The animals found it as their friend so good

The greens around found their support to live
Unhindered and unbounded it's there to give
Emotional and practical support always came
Form the clear conscience of it without any claim

The residents and wayfarers come and go
To quench their thirst from their friend they know
Which is eternal without any bill of restaurant
So cool and calm with it's heart always flamboyant.

AMAR VALOBASAR ASHA

by Dr.Human for humanity on April 5, 2022.
© Dr. Hemendra Kumar Mandal, All rights reserved
Ami aaj boro akla
Amar din raat sondhyabalay
Thake nirjon noyoner jolfala
Amar hridoy ajke boroi nisso akla

Somoy Amar pase ese bose thomke ektu chay
Ami boli ki go tumi ki kichu bolbe amay
Se sudhu nischup bose thake
Ar amay opolok chokkhe dakhe

Din jay Maas jay bochoro chole jay
Moner majhe Amar nissota moneyei haray
Sokolei to hase kande anonde gaa vasay
Kintu ami to ta parini tobe ki amar jibon katbe emni obohalay?

THE MEDITATIVE AFTERNOON

by Dr.Human for humanity on April 6, 2022.
© Dr. Hemendra Kumar Mandal, All rights reserved
All people are gone for lunch ant take rest
In this opportunity the afternoon also started to meditate
The trees the sunshine the blue of the sky and the green
Produced an amazing and panoramic scene

The roads are now getting relaxation
from the heavyweight trailers superfast motion
The burning sun on the sky
Made everything almost fry

In this summer roads, trees, forests
No people or animals are wandering and takes rest
The trials thrown by the lives are getting tragic
Only relaxation can give protection from being sick.

KEY CHAIN

by Dr.Human for humanity on April 6, 2022.
© Dr. Hemendra Kumar Mandal, All rights reserved
Sometimes the key of my life
Is bound by a key chain of my bike
All on a sudden when I forgot the keys
The chain comes to me like God blessings

I need to tackle more than one keys
Of rooms, bike, cycle, car, flats in lease
So I need chains very much
Which can only save me as such

Once my key chain kept on the wall of the temple
Forgotten it without any clue not so simple
To find out as it was out from my mind
After long rushes by the God's grace I could find........

Author notes
100 words

WE ARE MULTI PERSONALITY 3 IN 1

by Dr.Human for humanity on April 6, 2022.
© Dr. Hemendra Kumar Mandal, All rights reserved
As we grow so also grows our personality
We become more and more clever losing integrity
Multi behaviors are the way we choose to follow
In our daily life sometimes we follow untruth
sometimes we don't go

The love hate and fear we always rear
In our daily lives without any tears
Sometimes love pulls the hate and backfire
In another they go hand in hand together

These musings are bearing multiple shades and colors
They Sometimes distracted with dilemma showers
But still they are the victims of cheating habits
Behaving as lioness but really they are rabbits.....

COFFEE AT THE ROOT OF MY BRAIN

by Dr.Human for humanity on April 6, 2022.
© Dr. Hemendra Kumar Mandal, All rights reserved
Yes when I am exhausted trying to read more
I need some coffee in my beverage store
I amcalone at the dead of night
My coffee as a friend helps me to fight

My uninvited tiredness then becomes light
Coffee is really a friend to diminish my plight

Author notes
6 lines

MY DOLLS CAME FROM MY LOVE

by Dr.Human for humanity on April 9, 2022.
© Dr. Hemendra Kumar Mandal, All rights reserved
We married many years passed
I found her dolls at last
Carefully packaged kept in the cupboard
Maintaining a nice and fine standard

I asked her what's the use of these
At such a distant time these will cease
Their relevance as nobody has time to take care
We are too busy to sit for and share

Her eyes were full of tears saying nothing
I asked again say what do you think
She told only a few words...memories of all
My family including you my first love still call

When at my pastime I remember those days
Gets vibrant and living always
In my mind the dolls run riots in my brain
And tries again and again for me to entertain.

SEX IS NOT A TABOO LIKE DRUGS

by Dr.Human for humanity on April 9, 2022.
© Dr. Hemendra Kumar Mandal, All rights reserved
I am a busy man but not an easy man
I don't think too much on a subject
As these go against my plan
Sex or no sex is not a thought to me as a poet

What makes me busy I go for that
It may be sex or anything for chat
My pleasure my joys my entertainment
Never depends solely on the sex bent

You may come as my lover
But that never guarantees your sex cover
Really it has no importance enough
As I don't think that over and above

My human touch to go for that
Only when it justify then Good or bad
Sadness or goodness I shall leave my work desk
To have your opinion on the wholesome sex

BUT STILL......

by Dr.Human for humanity on April 10, 2022.
© Dr. Hemendra Kumar Mandal, All rights reserved
Today I thought my best flower from the garden
I shall offer to my God with a pure heart not with a burden
So I went there with a pure prayer
My heart wanted to share

To my God the red hibiscus
But to my surprise when I plucked it with a flash
All on a sudden
it was dropped in the drain

I thought again and again
So cautious I had to maintain
So perfect you made it for your worshipping
But Alas at last it was refuted my dream

I thought for long why it happened
Even after my efforts to get
Your worship done
But at last your worship became undone

In this mortal world also
We plan for a dream or so
Plan for my love by force
But at last it results in divorce

I planned for growing money and protection
But at last it face rejection
All on a sudden without any notice
Breaking my mind and my minds peace.

EIGHTEEN NEEDS MORE FREEDOM

by Dr.Human for humanity on April 16, 2022.
© Dr. Hemendra Kumar Mandal, All rights reserved
I was under my fathers control in the family
Mother was in favor of more freedom nicely
But I was usually afraid of him
So that I could not pursue of some creative dream

I couldn't go to theaters or cinemas on my own
Father's permission and money was known
As the essential rule of thumb
Otherwise all were in vain and numb

No love no drinks no freedom of going astray
As he was tough enough to control my way
He was interested on my career
He was interested only about my shining future.

BIDEN ALSO BORN BY A DRAIN

by Dr.Human for humanity on April 19, 2022.
© Dr. Hemendra Kumar Mandal, All rights reserved
Like every politicians I hate Biden
As they are motivated always by a selfish end
Trump was rejected for a better one
But people seen the drastic defeat from useless Taliban

Was it the target of the people ?
Biden made them utter fool
So now Americans have to keep their cool
As everybody to be elected are unqualified to rule

Trump was forcefully shown the door
As people expected from Biden more
But all in vain now wait for four more years
And let him give you far more tears

He is Nato head but sold himself to Russian Putin
For fuel purchase made the people unseen
So politician are bore
The should be entertained any more

POETRY DOESN'T DEPEND ON A PARTICULAR MONTH

by Dr.Human for humanity on April 26, 2022.
© Dr. Hemendra Kumar Mandal, All rights reserved
Poetry as well as Poets are universal
You can't bind it with cords which are colossal
It has got a mind greater than the sky
You can't touch it whatever you go to a high

The beauty the duty the lovers warm touch
Poetry is always advanced too much
To find peace for you and others
It has no trifling thought which bothers

Even at the time of wars of children of civilization
Poets think of a new world order in motion
They cry they try for all the best
So that no effort for peace doesn't become waste

Poets are cool colored and beautiful
Always think of Joy with their tool
They think out of our civilization
A utopia coming out of heaven of a cool automation

THE BIKE ACCIDENT

by Dr.Human for humanity on May 2, 2022.
© Dr. Hemendra Kumar Mandal, All rights reserved
The last Thursday I was rushing with my bike
From the evening prayer of Ramkrishna mission
I got a havoc and indelible strike
With two violently rushing dogs with lightning motion

Came over the road just in front of my bike
I was in utter dismay violently made to strike
The bulky quarreling dog within a fraction of a second
The most violent accident in my lifetime found

My bleeding left and right hands and orthopedic wound
Made me awkward and unsound
People gave me water and wounds are washed by them
They came like Samaritans and I thought them to be godsend

But alas I couldn't found the dog anywhere
The violently fled one after the strike
I must say his wound must hsve been more
Than those of me with my bike

May God keep him cool and in good shape
As I have many treatments to gather
But he is a street dog of healthy make
But still he need a great care.......

MY THOUGHTS FOR YOU CHANGED ME FOREVER ???

by Dr.Human for humanity on May 2, 2022. © Dr. Hemendra Kumar Mandal, All rights reserved

I was walking through the street
To get the day's unusual heat
When my rushing eye got the beat
From your cool breeze so sweet

The day was the turning point
My rushes for anything got cool
My brain got lots of ice as if to join
Your smile with its working tool

The day I never forgot
As it was only the beauty spot
Of my ugly life before
Scattered thereafter flowers more and more

My mind received a kind of meditation
Your thoughts got all the attention
Which got me sometimes astray
But Scattered flowers always all my way......

Author notes

101 words

TO BE THE DEAR BE OUT OF FEAR

by Dr.Human for humanity on May 2, 2022. © Dr. Hemendra Kumar Mandal, All rights reserved
Everything you ever wanted is on the other side of FEAR...George Addais

To go beyond the sky
you must be a mountain high
You need not see the downside
You must move with dauntless pride

Fear itself is a negative vibe
It always tries to get you out of life
No hope no scope no pleasure anymore
Fear is the depth of the sea not the seashore

To enjoy boundless
You must confess
And go out of your den
That you are fearless

The more the doubts
The fearsome whereabouts
Are dangerous distractions
Destroy lives all attractions

OUR ENCOUNTER WITH UNPRECEDENTED HAPPINESS

by Dr.Human for humanity on May 13, 2022. © Dr. Hemendra Kumar Mandal, All rights reserved
One day on a winter night
Some social workers from my friends
Seen some beggars with great plight
Distributing rags to them within their sight

Everything was normal everybody got rags
Everybody was happy to get their happy tags
But within them one was different an old man
His words were extraordinary and he was their fan

But before taking he told 'you can give me one '
If you have two for me otherwise distribute my piece to the other sick one
They were astonished to see
Because his happiness is not for him only

It depends on the other people who is more sick
So to feel needs of others he is was very quick
The Samaritans felt at the dead of night
What is happiness and what is love and light

We read books and periodicals
We hear sermons from the mountains
But can we feel like that poor man
What is happiness What is a good Samaritan?

www.ingramcontent.com/pod-product-compliance
Lightning Source LLC
LaVergne TN
LVHW061545070526
838199LV00077B/6907